W9-AOF-168

HOW It's MADE

A Paper Bag

Sue Barraclough

GARETH**STEVENS**
GS
PUBLISHING
A Member of the WRC Media Family of Companies

Please visit our web site at: www.garethstevens.com
For a free color catalog describing Gareth Stevens Publishing's list of high-quality books
and multimedia programs, call 1-800-542-2595 (USA) or 1-800-387-3178 (Canada).
Gareth Stevens Publishing's fax: (414) 332-3567.

Library of Congress Cataloging-in-Publication Data

Barraclough, Sue.
   A paper bag / Sue Barraclough.
      p. cm. — (How it's made)
   ISBN-10: 0-8368-6703-3 — ISBN-13: 978-0-8368-6703-9 (lib. bdg.)
   1. Paper bags—Juvenile literature.   2. Papermaking—Juvenile literature.   I. Title.   II. Series.
TS1200.B37   2006
676`.287—dc22   2006042294

This North American edition first published in 2007 by
Gareth Stevens Publishing
A Member of the WRC Media Family of Companies
330 West Olive Street, Suite 100
Milwaukee, WI 53212 USA

This U.S. edition copyright © 2007 by Gareth Stevens, Inc.
Original edition copyright © 2006 by Franklin Watts.
First published in Great Britain in 2006 by Franklin Watts,
338 Euston Road, London NW1 3BH, United Kingdom.

Series editor: Sarah Peutrill
Art director: Jonathan Hair
Designer: Jemima Lumley

Gareth Stevens editor: Tea Benduhn
Gareth Stevens art direction: Tammy West
Gareth Stevens graphic designer: Charlie Dahl

Photo credits: (t=top, b=bottom, l=left, r=right, c=center)
Alamy: front cover br, l, 4tl, 27br. Bettmann/CORBIS: 23tr. Brand X/Alamy: 22br. Dr. Jeremy Burgess/SPL: 7t. CORBIS:
25b. Colin Crisford/Alamy: 22bl. Mark Edwards/Still Pictures: 19b. Forest Stewardship Council: 31c. David R. Frazier
Photolibrary Inc./Alamy: 17, 26br. Tommaso Guicciardini/SPL: 13t, 26tr. Robert Harding PL: 23tl. Brownie Harris/CORBIS:
24t. Jacqui Hurst/CORBIS: 14. R. Maisonneuve/Publiphoto Diffusion/SPL: 16cl. Hans Pfetschinger/Still Pictures: 13b.
Popperfoto: 9b. Charles O. Rear/CORBIS: 9tl. Alex Segre/Rex Features: 21, 27tl. Friedrich Stark/Still Pictures: 16br. Stora
Enso (Lasse Arvidsson and Birger Roos): front cover c, back cover both, 4tr, 4b, 5t, 6t, 6b, 7b, 8, 9tr, 10t, 11tl, 11tr, 11b, 12t, 15t,
15b, 18, 19t, 20t, 20b, 22t, 26tl, 26cl, 26bl, 26cr, 27bl, 27cl, 30l, 30r, 31t. Kaj R. Svensoson/SPL: 12b. Visions of America,
LLC/Alamy: 10b. Werner Forman Archive/Topfoto: 5b. Every effort has been made to trace the copyright holders for the
photos used in this book. The publisher apologizes, in advance, for any unintentional omissions and would be pleased to
insert the appropriate acknowledgements in any subsequent edition of this publication.

Printed in the United States of America

1 2 3 4 5 6 7 8 9 10 09 08 07 06

Words that appear in the glossary are printed in
boldface type the first time they occur in the text.

Contents

This bag is made of paper.

Paper bags like this one are made to carry items purchased from stores.

The story of a paper bag starts with living, growing trees. Most paper is made from the wood from trees.

Forests provide wood, which we use to make paper.

Why paper?

Paper is a product that has many uses. It can be made from wood, fabric, or the fibers of plants. It can be **recycled**, and it is **biodegradable**, which means that it will rot away or break down until it is gone.

Can you imagine the **process** that makes smooth, flexible paper from hard, rough trees?

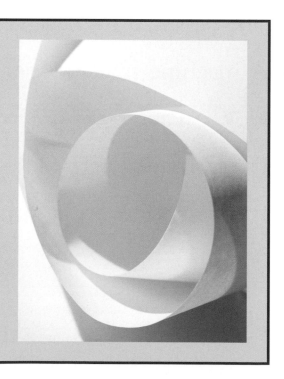

Some types of wood are better for making paper than others. Trees that provide papermaking wood are specially grown on plantations. A plantation is an area of trees planted in tidy rows. People also plant papermaking trees in **semi-natural forests.**

Pine trees can be planted close together because they grow tall and straight.

In the Past

Ancient Egyptians made the earliest kind of paper from the papyrus plant. They glued together very thin slices of the plant to form sheets.

Egyptians made this sheet of paper in about 1295–1186 B.C.

Historians think a man named Ts'ai Lun may have been the first to make paper from fiber pulp in A.D. 105, in China. Ts'ai Lun made his paper from hemp, the bark of a mulberry tree, and scraps of linen and cotton. He mashed the fibers and mixed them with water. Then he pressed the fiber pulp into mats and left the mats of pulp to dry in the sun. Papermaking spread all over Asia and finally to Europe in about A.D. 1009. The French and Italians then led the paper industry from 1250 to 1470. The first U.S. paper mill opened in Philadelphia in 1690.

Workers plant trees to use for papermaking.

Tree plantations grow just one type of tree because trees are easy to look after when they are all the same type.

Tiny eucalyptus seedlings grow in this greenhouse.

This worker is planting seedlings.

When workers cut down trees, they replace them with new trees. Plantations usually have trees at different stages of growth. Some trees are big enough to be cut down. Other trees are small and still growing. There are also greenhouses with tiny seedlings beginning to grow. Workers plant the seedlings in areas where trees have been cut down.

Some trees, such as eucalyptus trees, grow much faster than others. Trees that grow fast are often grown for papermaking.

This tiny eucalyptus tree will grow fast, straight, and tall. The tree will grow for about eight years, and then it will be big enough to be used for papermaking.

You can see the difference between areas of natural, mixed forest and neatly planted rows of eucalyptus trees in this plantation in Brazil.

In the Past
Until the mid-1800s, paper was made from recycled materials such as linen and cotton rags. Paper was made in small amounts, and it was a lot more rare than it is today.

The trees are cut down and chopped up.

Some types of trees produce hardwood, and others produce softwood. The hard and soft wood make different types of paper. Hardwood trees include eucalyptus and birch, while softwoods are produced by trees such as pine and spruce.

A harvester machine cuts down trees and chops them into lengths. It then sorts the chopped trees into hardwood and softwood piles.

This harvester can do several jobs. It cuts down the tree, chops it into lengths, and sorts it into piles.

The sorted logs are then transported by road, rail, or water to pulp mills.

Cranes load heavy logs onto trucks.

Tugboats move a huge raft of logs down a river.

In the Past

In the 1840s, when trees became more widely used to make paper, lumber camps sprang up wherever there were large areas of forest. Men flocked to these camps to work as lumberjacks. The lumberjacks chopped down each tree with an ax or a saw.

This lumberjack from the 1950s holds an ax.

Paper is made from wood fibers.

To make pulp, all the fibers that form the wood need to be broken down and separated. The fibers are put back together in a different way to form paper.

The fibers in wood make it strong and hard. This wood has to be broken down to make paper.

bark (on the outside)

each ring shows one year's growth

These huge logs need to have their bark removed.

At the pulp mill, logs are sprayed with water and put into large drums. The drums turn and tumble the logs against each other until they are stripped of their rough, outer layer of bark.

Then the logs go into a chipper, which cuts them down into small squares called wood chips.

These wood chips are ready for the next stage.

At a pulp mill, huge mountains of wood chips are processed day and night.

Why wood?

Wood is widely used for papermaking because it is easily available, and it is the best material for the job. Different types of wood pulp can be used to produce a range of different papers, from thick cardboard to thin tissue paper. Hardwoods such as birch and eucalyptus have short fibers, which make smooth paper. Softwoods such as pine and spruce have long fibers, which make strong paper. Papermakers often combine hardwood and softwood to make strong, smooth paper.

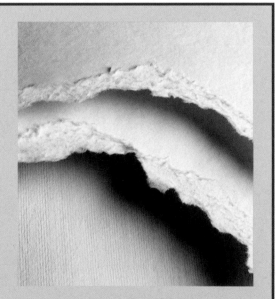

You can see the fibers in this torn paper.

Water, chemicals, and heat turn wood chips into pulp.

A gluelike substance called lignin holds together wood fibers. The lignin must be removed in order to separate the fibers.

Wood chips are fed into a digester, which separates the fibers.

Networks of pipes bring water, chemicals, and other ingredients into the pulpmaking process.

The wood chips are mixed with water and **chemicals** and heated in big, metal containers called **digesters**.

The heat and chemicals melt the lignin and turn the wood chips into a porridge-like pulp.

Wood chips are made into a mushy pulp.

In the Past

French scientist Rene de Reaumur may have come up with the idea of using wood fibers to make paper in 1719. He watched a wasp making its nest, and he noticed how the wasp turned small pieces of wood into a paper paste. Many people, however, think that all the credit goes to the Chinese.

These paper wasps use the same basic recipe to make their nests as people use for making paper. The paper wasps chew small pieces of wood. They mix the wood with their saliva to make a paste. Then they mold the paste to make their nests.

The pulp is bleached.

Bleaching makes the pulp white. Papers made for printing are usually bleached. Some pulp is not bleached and may be used to make brown grocery bags and cardboard boxes. The bag on the cover of this book is white, so it is made from bleached pulp. Other ingredients can also be added to wood pulp to make different types of paper. The ingredients are added to give the paper texture or color or to make it stronger. Sometimes, recycled pulp is also added.

The paper pulp is brown. This pulp will be bleached white with a gas called oxygen.

The papermaker decides on a mixture of pulps to make a paper bag. He or she mixes the pulps to make sure the paper bag has the right strength and will not split easily.

sheets of paper

bleached pulp

Pulp goes through many stages to be made into paper. This picture shows bleached pulp.

Why recycle paper?

By recycling paper, we use up fewer trees. We also use less energy and water and create less **pollution**. Most of the paper that people use can be collected, sorted, and turned into recycled fiber. Some strong, new tree fiber is also added to the pulp at the paper mill because repeated recycling weakens the fibers. Recycling paper helps save forests and is environmentally friendly.

Some pulp mills now use recycled paper as their main source of material.

The pulp is checked before it is taken to the paper mill.

Papermakers check the quality of the paper at every stage of the process. They take samples to make sure the pulp has the right properties.

A worker takes a sample of pulp.

Then the pulp is ready to go to the paper mill. At the mill, papermakers mix the pulp with more water to make **slurry**. The slurry is thinner than pulp and easier to spread out evenly.

Traditional Papermaking

Traditional methods of making paper are still used in many parts of the world. This woman is draining water from paper pulp. A sheet of paper is starting to form in the tray.

Next, the slurry goes into the **headbox**. This part of the machine spreads the mixture evenly onto a quickly moving wire-mesh tray. The papermaking machine then removes most of the water.

Some water drops out of the slurry through the wire mesh tray. Rollers squeeze more water out of the leftover mixture. The last of the pulp is pressed between materials that soak up even more water.

The wet paper pulp, called slurry, is spread onto a large wire tray.

The paper is pressed and dried.

In the press section, the fibers are pressed together tightly. Pressing removes water and increases the strength of the paper. In the drying section, the sheets are dried with steam-heated cylinders.

Next, the size press, which is a machine used for coating paper, covers the paper with a thin layer of starch. The starch coating stops printing inks from soaking into the paper.

Paper reels through the size press for a coating of starch.

The paper then goes through the **calender** section. The calender is a machine with polished steel rolls that press the paper. The calender uses heat and pressure to make the paper the same thickness all over. The paper is then reeled into jumbo rolls.

The paper is now in a jumbo roll.

Traditional Papermaking

After paper pulp bonds together to make paper, the bonded pulp needs to be pressed and then dried. In traditional papermaking, the sheets of paper are hung on a line to dry — just like clothes.

In India, people handmake paper using traditional methods. They often use recycled paper pulp.

The jumbo rolls are sliced into smaller rolls.

Small rolls can be moved around the mill quickly.

Sheets of thick paper are wrapped around the sliced, small rolls to protect them. The paper is now ready to be transported to paper factories, printers, and paper merchants. The rolls can be cut down further to make small sheets for writing paper and envelopes. Whole rolls of paper are sent to printers to produce books and newspapers.

Papermakers carefully check and control every stage of the process at the paper mill.

Paper is also used for many types of packaging, such as boxes, milk cartons, wrappers, and bags. The paper for making bags is sent in big batches to the factory.

Trucks transport heavy rolls of paper to the paper bag manufacturer.

Why paper?

About half of all the paper produced worldwide is used in packaging. Paper is a popular material because it can be made into many different types of packaging. It can be soft, strong, lightweight, waterproof, or textured. It is also flexible, so it can be folded and molded into different shapes.

Recycled paper is often used for packaging papers. Another advantage of paper is that, unlike plastic, which is also popular for packaging, paper will rot when it is thrown away.

The paper bag is designed.

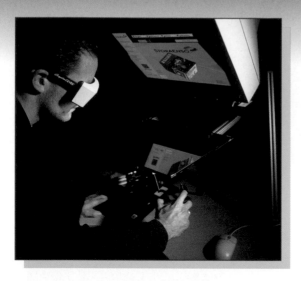

Designers use virtual packaging technology to test package designs on screen.

To produce a paper shopping bag, the designer chooses the paper and colors. The design of the bag needs to suit its purpose. If the bag needs to have handles, the designer decides how they will be added, and what material will be used to make them.

In the Past

Early shopkeepers used to wrap purchased items in paper, or maybe twist some paper into a cone to hold the items. Today, stores have many types of different bags, from simple brown paper bags to smart, brightly printed shopping bags.

This bag is a simple cylinder of paper, glued at one end.

Margaret Knight (1838–1914) invented a part for a machine to make a square-bottomed bag.

Paper and Printing

Gutenberg (*right*) is in his workshop.

Printing is important for some bags. Logos or patterns can advertise shops or products.

In 1453, German scientist Johann Gutenberg invented the moveable type printing press. The press was a turning point for papermaking. Now, books could be made quickly and inexpensively, so they became more widely available. As printing technology changed, the demand for paper grew. During the 1400s, rags were the main source of fiber, but there were not enough rags to make all the paper people wanted. Other materials, such as straw and hemp, were only harvested seasonally, so papermakers needed to find another source of fiber. Wood pulp, however, did not become widely used until the mid-1800s.

All these paper bags have different designs. They are all different shapes and sizes, and they have different handles.

A machine makes paper bags.

Once the designer finishes the design, a machine makes the paper bag. Bags can be made faster, neater, and more inexpensively by a machine than if they are made by hand.

A machine cuts paper into sheets that are the right size.

Sheets of paper go into one end of the paper bag machine and finished bags come out the other end.

As the paper goes through the machine, it is creased and folded.

The machine glues the bottom and sides of the paper to make the bag.

Handles are attached, one at a time, to each side.

The bags are folded flat and packed up. Then they are sent out to shops, ready to be used as shopping bags.

Many people carry paper bags when they go shopping.

How a Paper Bag Is Made

1. Trees grow in plantations, or they grow in semi-natural forests.

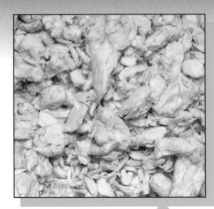

4. Water and heat turn the wood chips into a mushy pulp.

2. Trees are cut down, sorted, and transported. New trees are planted in their place.

5. The pulp is bleached.

3. Wood is chopped into small chips.

6. Water is added to the pulp to make slurry. The wet slurry is spread on a wire tray to drain it, and the drying process begins.

9. The jumbo roll is cut into smaller rolls, and the rolls are taken to the bag manufacturer.

10. The paper is cut and the paper bag is made in a machine.

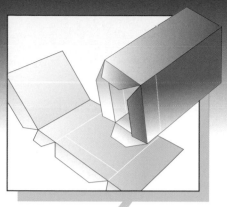

8. The calender uses heat and pressure to make paper the same thickness all over. Then the paper is reeled into jumbo rolls.

56t

11. The paper bag is ready to use. After it has been used, it can be recycled.

7. The paper reels through rollers. The fibers are pressed and stretched into sheets as they dry.

Paper and Its Many Uses

It is hard to imagine a world without paper. Think of all the everyday items we use, such as books, magazines, birthday cards, brochures, and posters. From tissues and toilet paper to cereal boxes and milk cartons, paper is everywhere in our homes.

Paper can be dyed with bright colors. This paper is smooth which makes it an ideal surface for writing or drawing.

Paper is light, and it is easy to bend and crease, so it makes perfect fans.

Paper can be used to make cartons like these.

Very thin paper lets light through, so it can be used to make shades for lamps.

Some paper is absorbent, which means it can soak up liquids. Paper towels soak up spills quickly and cleanly.

Two types of paper were used to make this dragon — thin tissue paper and thick cardboard.

The cardboard roll that holds this soft bathroom tissue is also made from paper.

Paper and the Environment

Trees are an important resource, which we can all help to protect.

Reducing Waste

Paper and wood companies do not waste any part of a tree that is cut down.

Managing Forests

Many paper companies manage forests responsibly. They plant a seedling for each tree they cut down or allow seeds that trees drop to grow naturally.

The smallest pieces of wood are used for **biofuel**.

Small trunk parts are used to make paper and **chipboard**.

Thicker parts of the trunk are used for timber and papermaking.

Sawmill leftovers are used to make paper and chipboard.

About 30 percent of the wood can be used for lumber products, and 70 percent of the wood can be used for pulp and paper.

Many places have recycling collection services.

We Can Help

Paper was once rare, but now it is made on a huge scale. It is inexpensive and widely available. The best way we can help is to use less paper and recycle what we do use.

Protecting Natural Forests

The Forest Stewardship Council (FSC) was founded to conserve the world's forests. Forests are vital for the well-being of Earth, but much of our natural forests have already been destroyed. The FSC makes sure that our remaining natural forests are left untouched and that plantations that produce wood are also managed well.

The other major forest certification organizations in North America and Europe are:
• The Sustainable Forest Initiative
• Canadian Standards Association
• The Programme for the Endorsement of Forest Certification Schemes

If you see this sign on wood, you know it has been taken from well managed forests.

Around the world many more organizations participate in conserving forests. About 5 percent of global forests have been certified as protected areas. In Western Europe and North America the number of certified forests is much higher at 30 to 50 percent.

Glossary

biodegradable − any material that can be broken down naturally in the environment

biofuel − fuel made from renewable raw materials such as bark and logging leftovers

calender − the machine that reels paper around steel rolls to make paper the same thickness all over

chemicals − substances that can make a change in other substances when they are mixed together

chipboard − a thin board made of wood chips that are pressed and glued together

digesters − containers that are used to heat and soften wood chips. Heating melts the lignin, a natural glue, which holds the wood fibers together.

headbox − a part at the start of a paper-making machine. It is a huge nozzle that spreads the paper pulp evenly onto a wire tray.

pollution − the condition of air, water, or land that has been made dirty or poisoned by harmful substances

process − a series of actions that produce a change

recycled − made into useful material from material that has already been used

semi-natural forests − forests that have grown naturally but are now partly managed by a business that plants and harvests trees

slurry − wet pulp that has more water added to it

Index